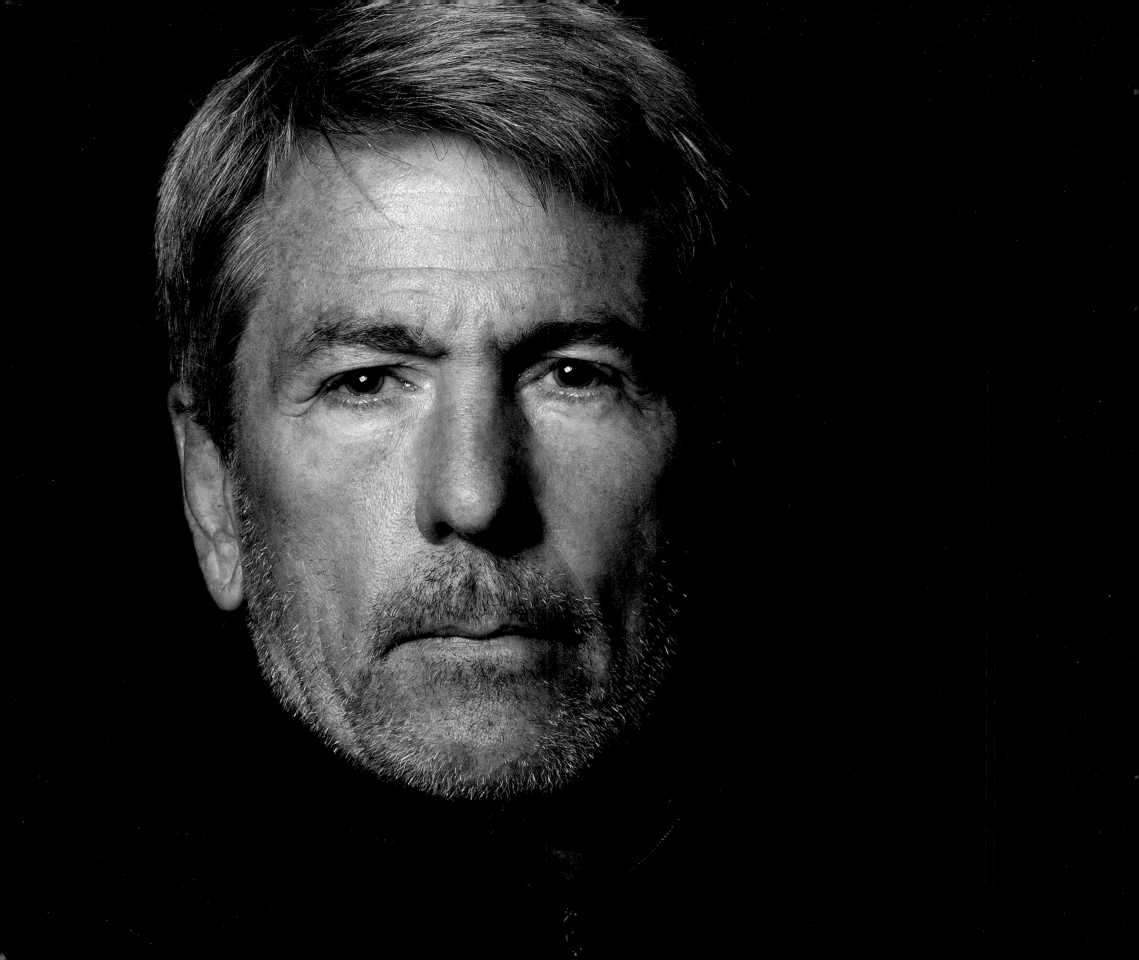

Born in Ohio, and raised in Short Hills, New Jersey, Robert Hooke is a graduate of Bowdoin College, and Columbia University, where he earned an MBA. After graduation, he joined the Navy during the Vietnam war. Commanding a SWIFT boat in the Mekong Delta, he earned a Bronze Star and the Navy Commendation Medal, both with the Combat V for Valor. Discharged as a full Lieutentant, he went to Wall Street, and subsequently to the City of London, where he managed the offices of DLJ, Paribas, and eventually, his own firm. While working in New York, he studied with Hertbert Kallem at the School for the Visual Arts. Kallem recognized Hooke's natural talent for stone carving, and gave him access to the school's studios at times that allowed him to work in finance during the day, and on his sculpture at nights and on weekends when the school was closed.

During his years in London, Hooke began to carve plaster and cast his work in bronze so he could produce multiple editions of his work. He started to show his work at the *Alwin Callery*, (which he later bought), as well as in galleries in Europe, Australia, and South Africa.

Jonathan Swift wrote, "He was a bold man that first ate an oyster", but perhaps a much bolder man was he who first took hammer and chisel to stone to create a work of art. One can always spit out an oyster, but a sculptor commited to a block of granite has no easy way out. And Hooke has been nothing if not bold. While many gentlemen may enjoy a round of golf, or perhaps a set or two of tennis, Hooke prefers something a bit more invigorating, such as racing solo around the world in a small sailboat, playing polo, sky diving, bungee jumping, heli-skiing, or big game hunting in South Africa.

That country, where Hooke maintains a second home, has had a great influence on his work. There he was able to observe African animals in the wild, and begin to understand their body language, something that can not be done in a zoo or learned from photographs. Hooke has always been more interested in stance than detail when sculpting animals, people or even plants. He likes to quote Miles Davis who said, "Creativity is not the notes you put in, but the ones you leave out".

Since 2009, when he returned to Sag Harbor, Hooke has continued to sculpt, showing his work in his own *Hooke Sculpture Gallery*, as well as galleries around the United States, Europe and South Africa.

Jonathan Morse   Sag Harbor 2011

The Duplicity of Language

By Eric Ernst

While the spoken world is considered humankind's most sophisticated form of communication, in many respects it pales in significance when compared to body language and posture as elemental mirrors reflecting reality's true narrative. Carrying nuances that transcend the subtleties of dialects or idioms as well as ripping away the masks we wear to diguise our perceptions or prejudices, stance and pose, as the performance artist Terry Galloway noted, illuminates the "duplicity that language is capable of and the many expressions the body cannot hide."

For the sculptor Robert Hooke, this emphasis on body language completely defines his focus of aesthetic priorities, whether it is in his studies of animals drawn from the natural world, or the interactive melodramas that echo through his use of the human form. Underscoring the concept that communication depends less on syntax than on sentiment or that stated expression is secondary to emotional sensation, Hooke elicits secrets from his silent figures by understating the obvious and emphasizing the inferred.

This relies on a number of factors ranging from an elemental understanding of Henry Moore's reference to "the form and shape of things", (what Emerson called the "anatomy of form"), to the recognition that an integral part of any sculpture, as Gertrude Stein observed, consisted of "some supports and pretty air". Underlying and emphasizing these singularly uncomplicated principles, however, is Hooke's abilitiy to understand that simplicity of the image itself is the most vital component in allowing the viewers to develop their own silent commuicative avenues between themselves and the scuptural object, (an effect accentuated by the lack of facial characteristics in any of the works).

This measure of simplicity is not, however, achieved simply through the indiscriminate and random expulsion of detail as if, in sculpting an angel, the process entailed merely chipping away everything that doesn't look angelic. Instead, through a practiced and intuitive sense of detached observation, the artist is able to understand the emotional structure of the object and thereby recreate not the actual reality of an image of something, but instead strive to emotively conjure the persona of the entity itself.

As a result, inevitable comparisons become apparent to these works and primitive art from Africa and elsewhere as viewers find themselves responding not simply on a visual level but also through the facility of imagination, emotion, and even some measure of mysticism, all aspects synonymous with primitive art. Further, Hooke's works are exemplified by a latent sense of formalism, a markedly subtle degree of pictorial sophistication, and an insistent exploration of emotional and psychological elments such as had existed as centuries old tradition of abstraction in African art long before its emergence in the west.
A significant difference, however, is that Hooke directs his focus more at figures and atmostpheric moments representing universally common emotional sensations, rather than using his figures to necessarily identify with some transcendent being or concept.

Whether reflected in the gentle camaraderie of "An Evening Walk",(marble), the wistfully meditative "Daydreamer", (bronze), or the rhythemically seductive "Flamenco Dancers", (bronze), Hooke draws inspiration from disparate elements of daily life while still imbuing the pose and posture of his subjects with an elegantly ethereal impassiveness.

This is also apparent in his works featuring animals from the natural world whose recreation is dependent not on aspects of scientific illustration nor the majestic idealizations of the nineteenth century "Animalier" artists. Instead in works such as "Leopard Head", (sandstone), "Monkeys", (bronze), or "Sleeping Swan", (alabaster), Hooke simplifies the forms so that planar dimensions are subtly softened and the materials themselves seem to yield the sense of existen-tiality, allowing the work to straddle the often intractable line in sculpture separating realism from abstraction.

Striving to balance modern impulses with traditional sensibilities and accentuating lines that are elegant in their unadorned minimalism, Robert Hooke is able to evoke profoundly memorable moments and emotions that are, by turns, both unique and universal. He arrives at this with a recognition that image, form, and narrative are intrinsically intertwined and that their complexities are best understood when stripped of all needless embellishments and adornments. In effect, searching for their emotive and spiritual essence by subtracting the superfluous and spurious, thereby reflecting Hans Hoffman's observation that one must "eliminate the unnecessary so that the necessary may speak."

TABLE OF CONTENTS

BIOGRAPHY by Jonathan Morse

INTRODUCTION by Eric Ernst

STONE SCULPTURE
    ANIMALS
    FIGURES

BRONZE SCULPTURE
    ANIMALS
    BIRDS
    FIGURES

PLANTS

STONE ANIMALS

Stone Animals

African Elephant
14 x 16 x 11"   Marble

Baboon Head
12 x 14 x 7"   Soapstone

Baboon Head Verso
12 x 14 x 7"   Soapstone

Horse Torso
10 x 9 x 3"   Marble

Leopard Head
6 x 8 x 9"   Marble

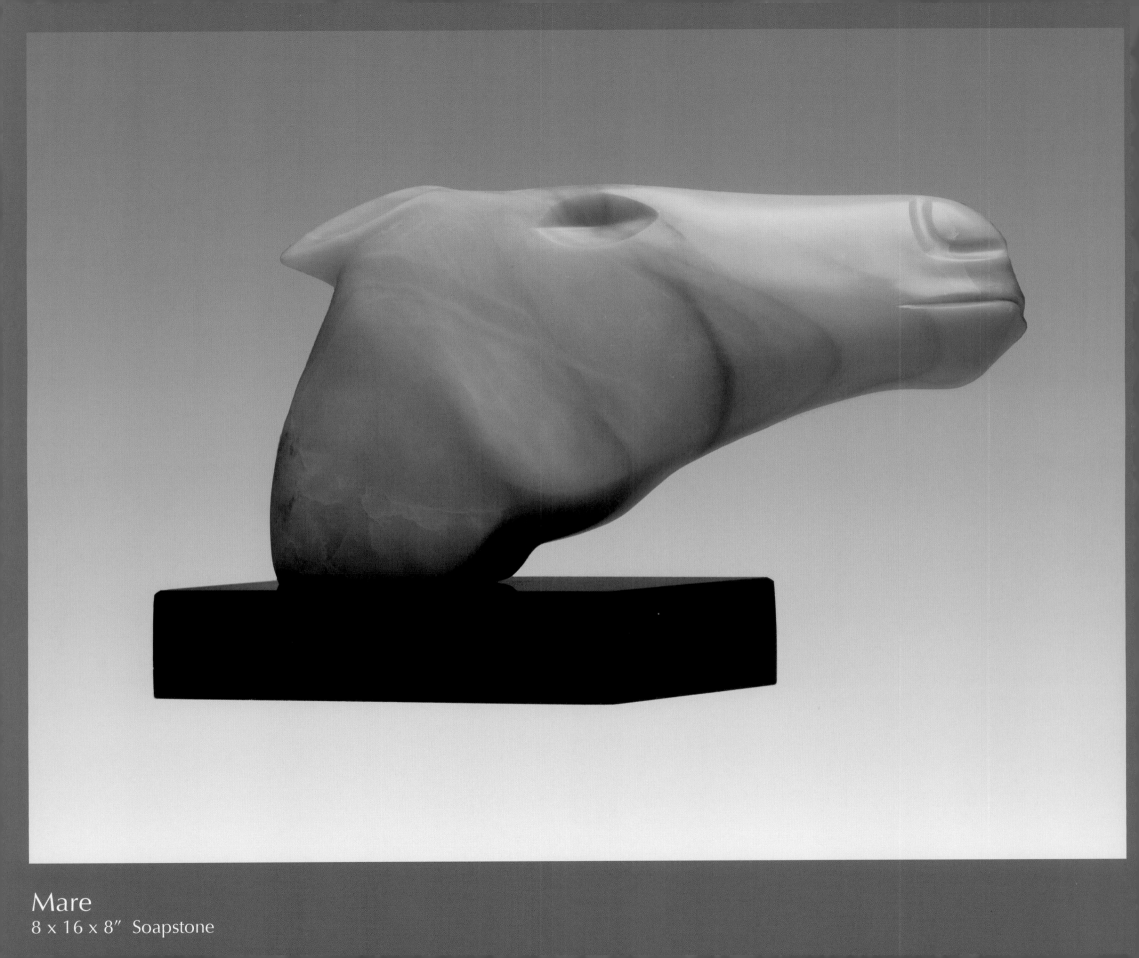

Mare
8 x 16 x 8" Soapstone

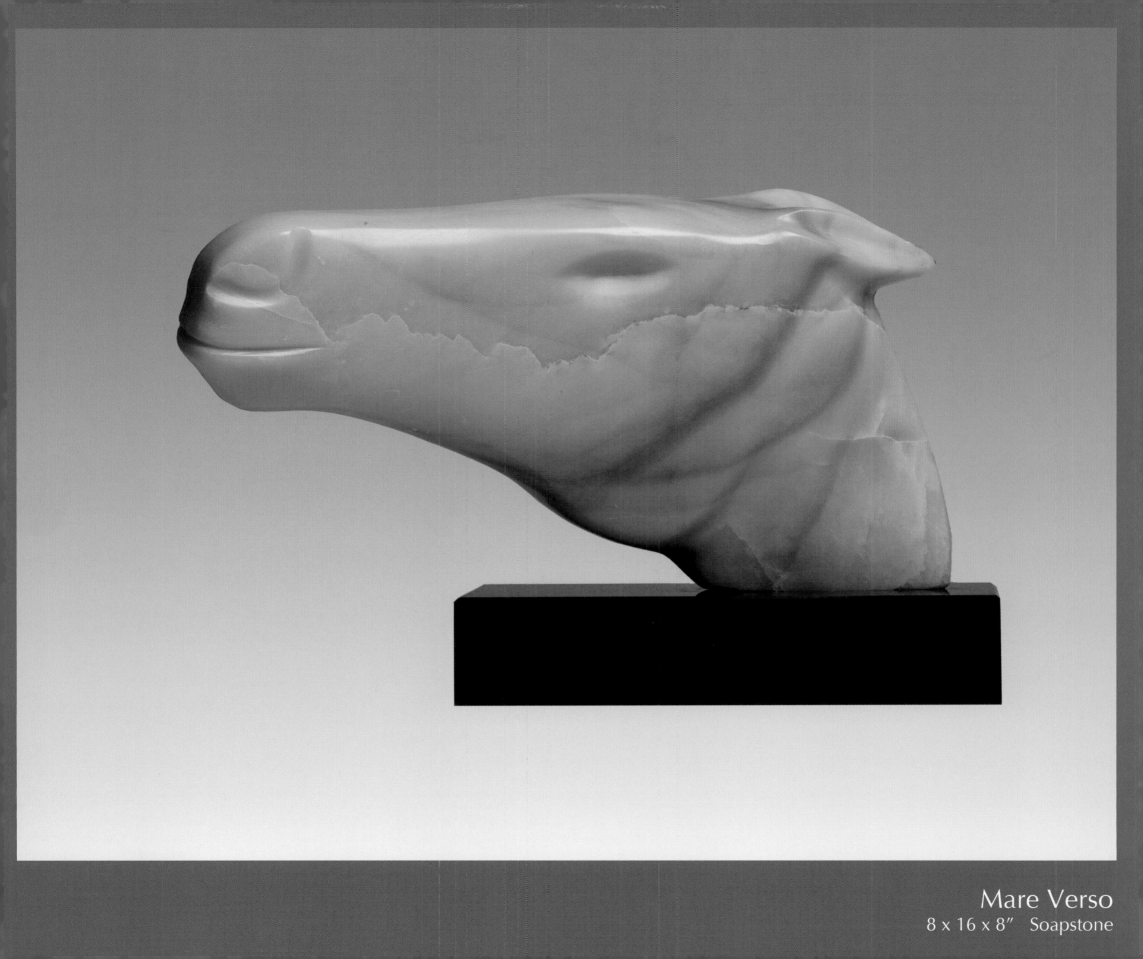

Mare Verso
8 x 16 x 8"   Soapstone

Swan Head
6 x 14 x 7"   Soapstone

Sleeping Swan
7 x 12 x v5″   Alabaster

Stallion
7 x 16 x 7"   Soapstone

Stallion Verso
7 x 16 x 7"   Soapstone

Lion Head
16 x 18 x 7"   Soapstone

Lion Head Verso
16 x 18 x 7"   Soapstone

Young Friends
7 x 1 0 x 8" Marble

Lioness
8 x 17 x 4" Marble

STONE FIGURES

STONE FIGURES

Expectant Mother
13 x 7 x 7"   Alabaster

Ballet Dancer
17 x 17 x 8" Marble

Coverup
29 x 9 x 9" Marble

Dancers
20 x 6 x 15"   Marble

Crossed Arms
14 x 6 x 4" Marble

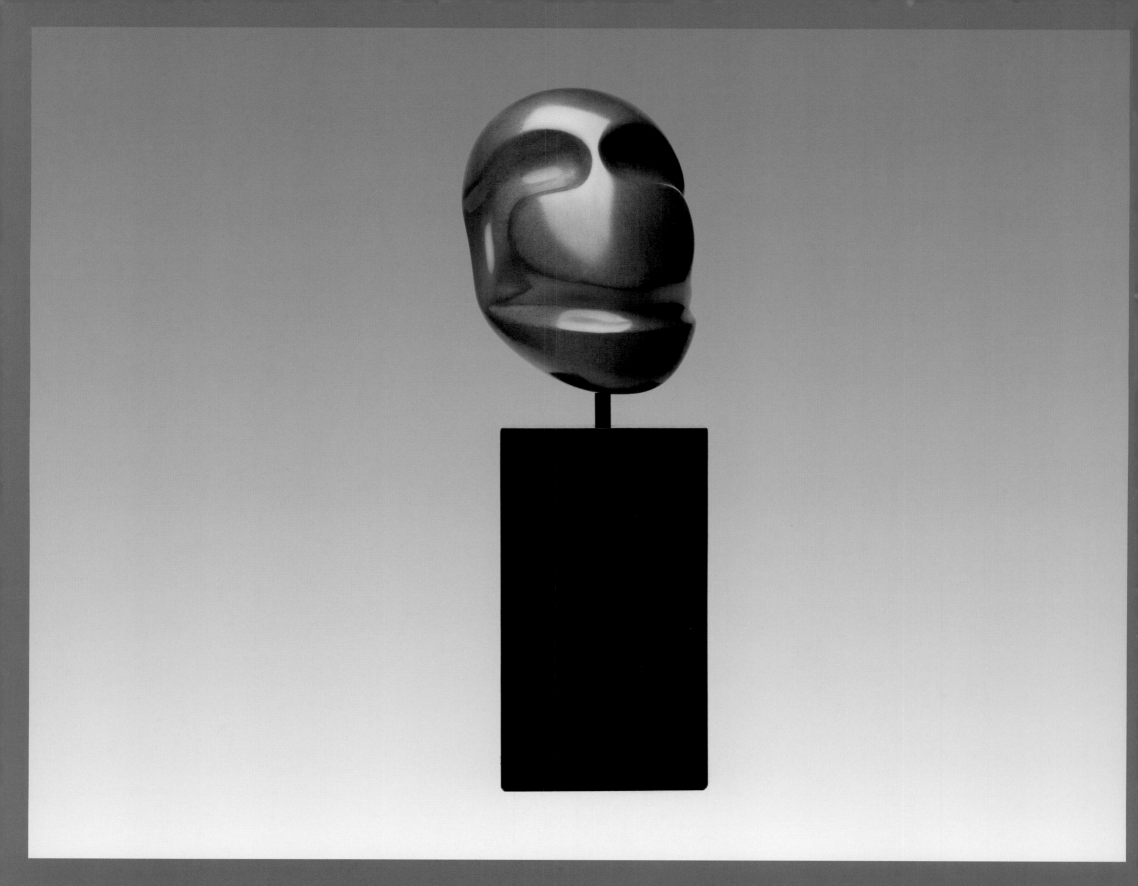

Skull
14 x 5 x 7"   African Wonderstone

Mask

9 x 6 x 4"   Soapstone

Thinking Man
31 x 8 x 10" Marble

Polka
16 x 12 x 8"   Soapstone

Running Man
8 x 11 x 7"   Alabaster

Mother and Child
13 x 12 x 7"   Soapstone

Walking Woman
13 x 7 x 6"   Marble

Evening Walk
12 x 8 x 4"   Onyx

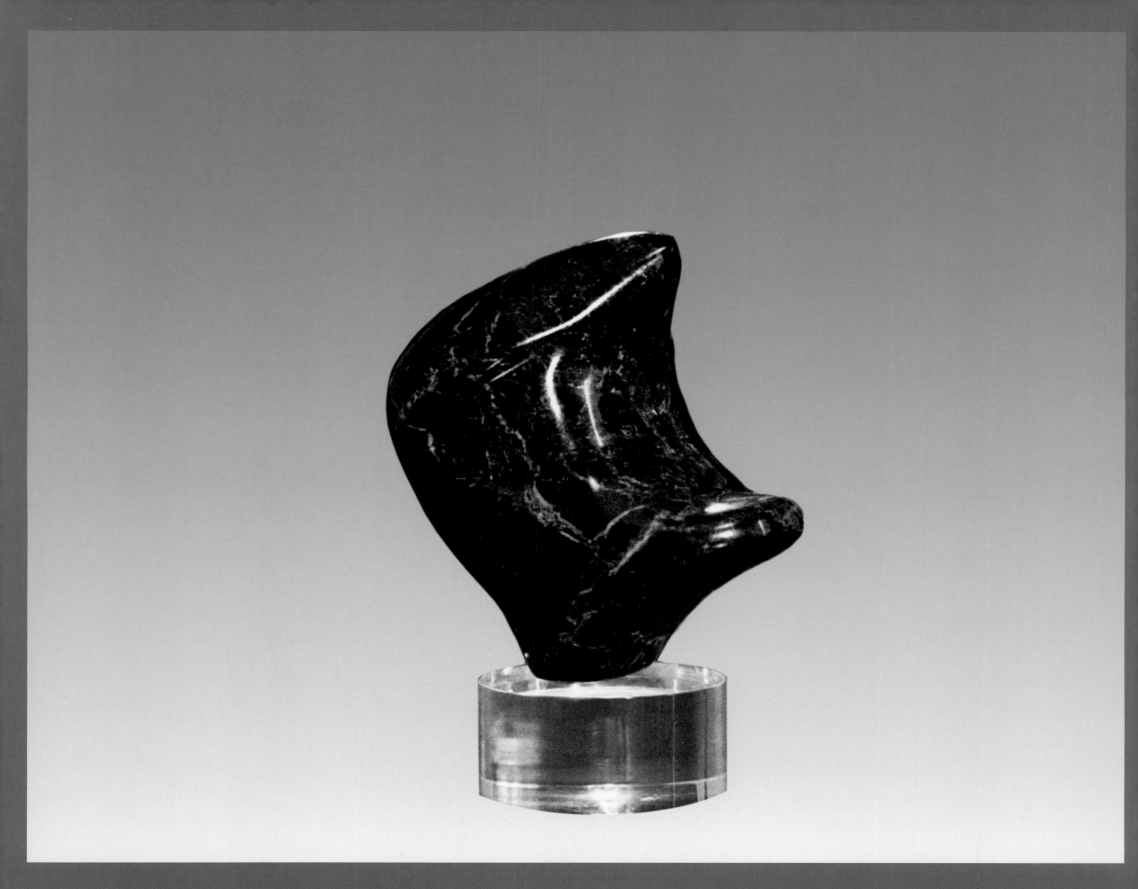

Head 1
14 x 10 x 8"   Marble

Surprise!
25 x 7 x 4"   Marble

Waiting
12 x 8 x 4" Alabaster

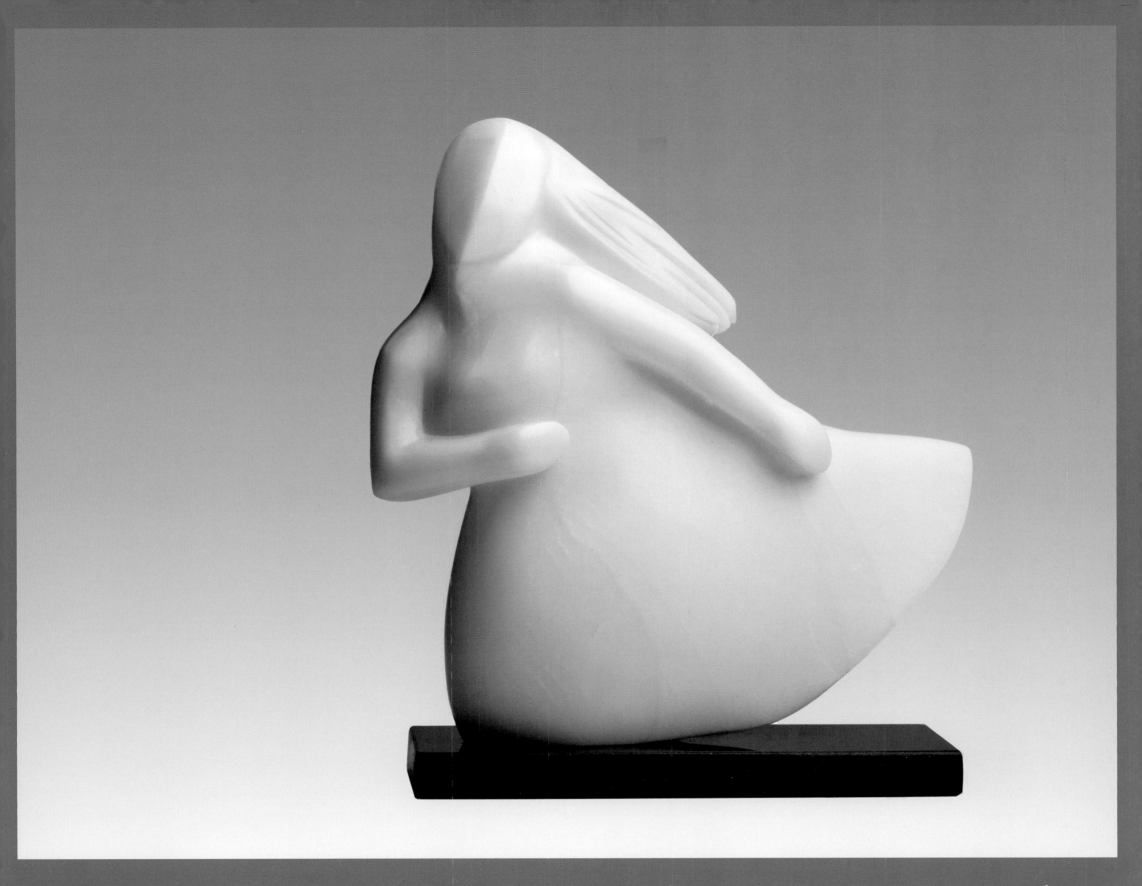

Windswept
12 x 11 x 16" Soapstone

BRONZE ANIMALS

BRONZE ANIMALS

Cheetah Running
8 x 20 x 5"   Bronze Edition of 6

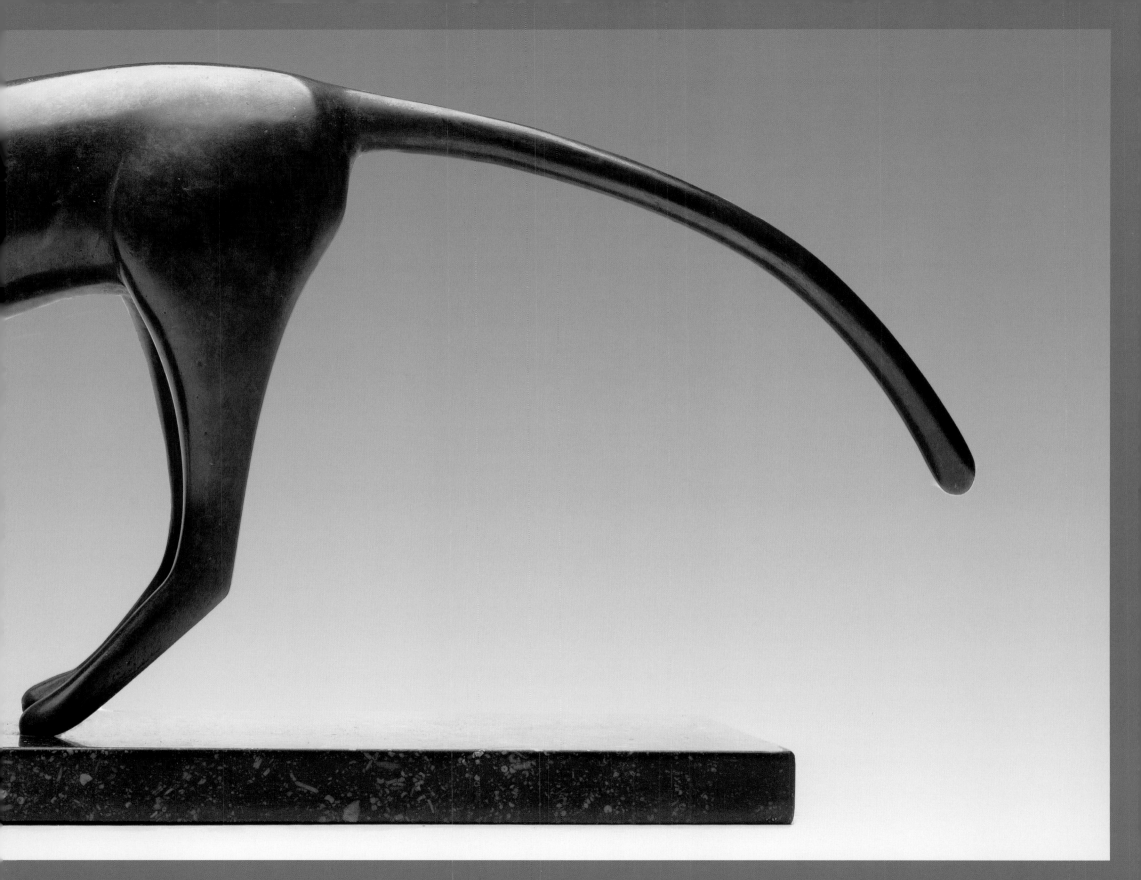

Cheetah Running
8 x 20 x 5" Bronze Edition of 9

Leopard Preening
8 x 9 x 5" Bronze Edition of 6

Panther Stalking
6 x 13 x 3" Bronze Edition of 6

Tiger
10 x 20 x 6″   Bronze Edition of 9

Hippo
9 x 19 x 6" Bronze Edition of 9

Bear Head
11 x 12 x 12" Bronze Edition of 9

African Elephant
12 x 14 x 10 "   Bronze Edition of 8

Bison
8 x 13 x 5"   Bronze Edition of 9

Zebra
9 x 13 x 4"   Bronze   Edition of 6

Kudu Bull
18 x 15 x 3"   Bronze Edition of 6

Giraffe
20 x 12 x 4" Bronze Edition of 4

Monkeys
9 x 9 x 6"   Bronze Edition of 6

Baboons
6 x 12 x 6"   Bronze   Edition of 9

Jaguar
8 x 18 x 4" Bronze Edition of 9

Lions

9 x 19 x 9"   Bronze Edition of 6

Colt
10 x 20 x 6"   Bronze   Edition of 9

Stallion
14 x 22 x 6"   Bronze Edition of 9

Mare (Verso)
18 x 16 x 8"   Bronze Edition of 9

Mare
18 x 16 x 8"   Bronze Edition of 9

Wild Dog
8 x 10 x 4" Bronze Edition of 9

African Wild Dogs
8 x 15 x 10"   Bronze   Edition of 9

Horse and Rider
12 x 19 x 7" Bronze Edition of 9

Rhino

6 x 12 x 4"   Bronze   Edition of 6

Leopard Hunting
7 x 14 x 5"   Bronze Edition of 6

Fox

6 x 12 x 3"   Bronze   Edition of 9v

Shark
14 x 12 x 6"   Bronze Edition of 5

Stablemates
9 x 18 x 7" Bronze Edition of 9

Sleeping Dog
4 x 13 x 8"   Bronze   Edition of 9

Polar Bear
10 x 20 x 6"   Bronze   Edition of 9

Polar Bear Head
9 x 18 x 8" Bronze Edition of 9

Mutt

6 x 9 x 3"   Bronze Edition of 3

Cheetah Leaping
9 x 22 x 3" Bronze Edition of 9

Sable Antelope
16 x 17 x 4"   Bronze Edition of 6

BRONZE BIRDS

Bronze Birds

Eagle Owl
36 x 12 x 10"   Bronze   Edition of 9

Falcon
18 x 4 x 4"   Bronze Edition of 6

Macaw

18 x 6 x 9" Bronze Edition of 3

Gull Flying
10 x 17 x 34"   Bronze Edition of 6

Gull Gliding

6 x 37 x 16" Bronze Edition of 6

Heron Alert
28 x 12 x 12"   Bronze Edition of 9

Heron Preening
28 x 12 x 12" Bronze Edition of 9

Swan
12 x 13 x 5"   Bronze   Edition of 6

Young Flamingo
33 x 18 x 8"   Bronze Edition of 9

Flamingo
57 x 18 x 12"   Bronze Edition 0f 6

Daydreamer
5 x 20 x 7"   Bronze Edition of 4

Flamenco Dancers Left
Man 37x12x12"   Woman 39x12x12"   Bronze Edition of 3

Flamenco Dancers Right
Man 37x12x12″   Woman 39x12x12″   Bronze   Edition of 3

Friends (Verso)
15 x 9 x 5"   Bronze Edition of 3

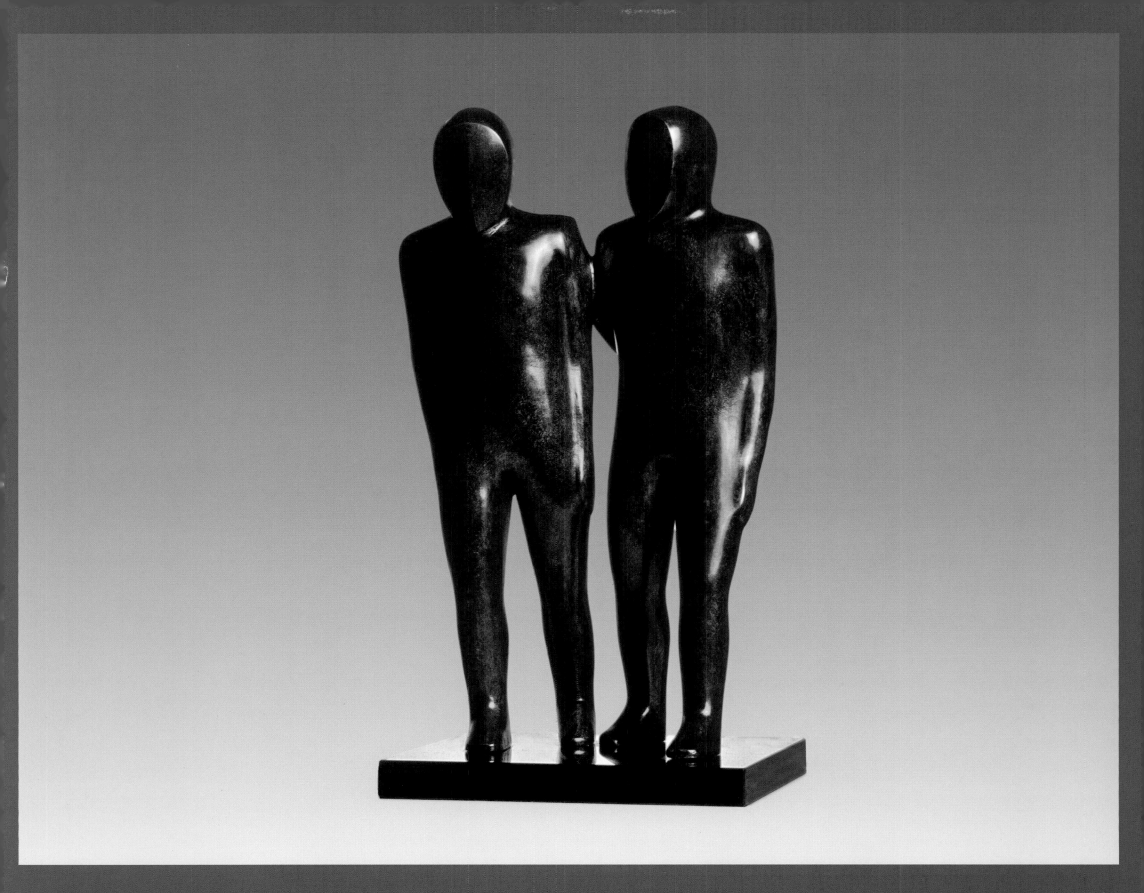

Friends
15 x 9 x 5" Bronze Edition of 3

Kneeling Man
12 x 5.5 x 11" Bronze edition of 4

Military Group
12 x 12 x 12" Bronze Edition of 3

Reclining Woman
6 x 10 x 3" Bronze Edition of 4

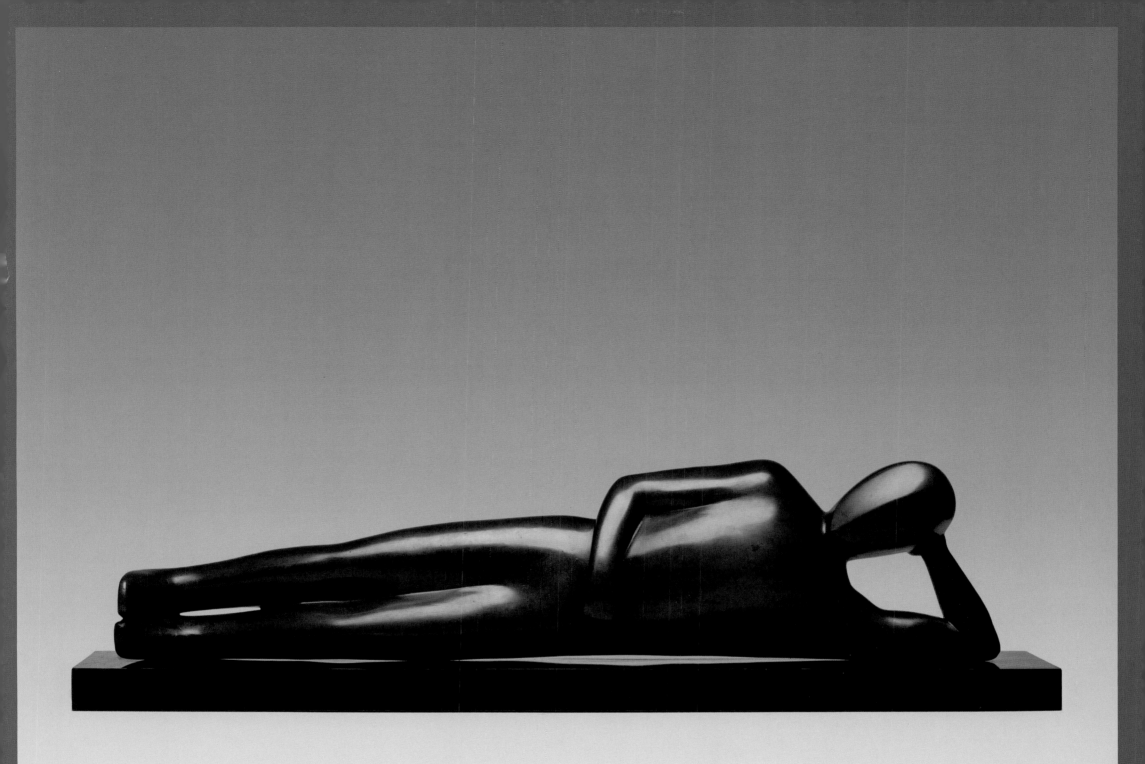

Reclining Man
7 x 27 x 4" Bronze Edition of 4

Seated Woman
12 x 6 x 10" Bronze   Edition of 5

Rendevous ll
7 x 21 x 14" Bronze Edition of 9

Standing Woman
64 x 15 x 9"   Bronze Edition of 9

Rendevous 1
Life Size and 19 x 7 x 5″ Bronze Editions of 9

Running Man
15 x 5 x 3" Bronze Edition of 3

Rendezvous 3
15 x 10 x 6″ Bronze Edition of 9

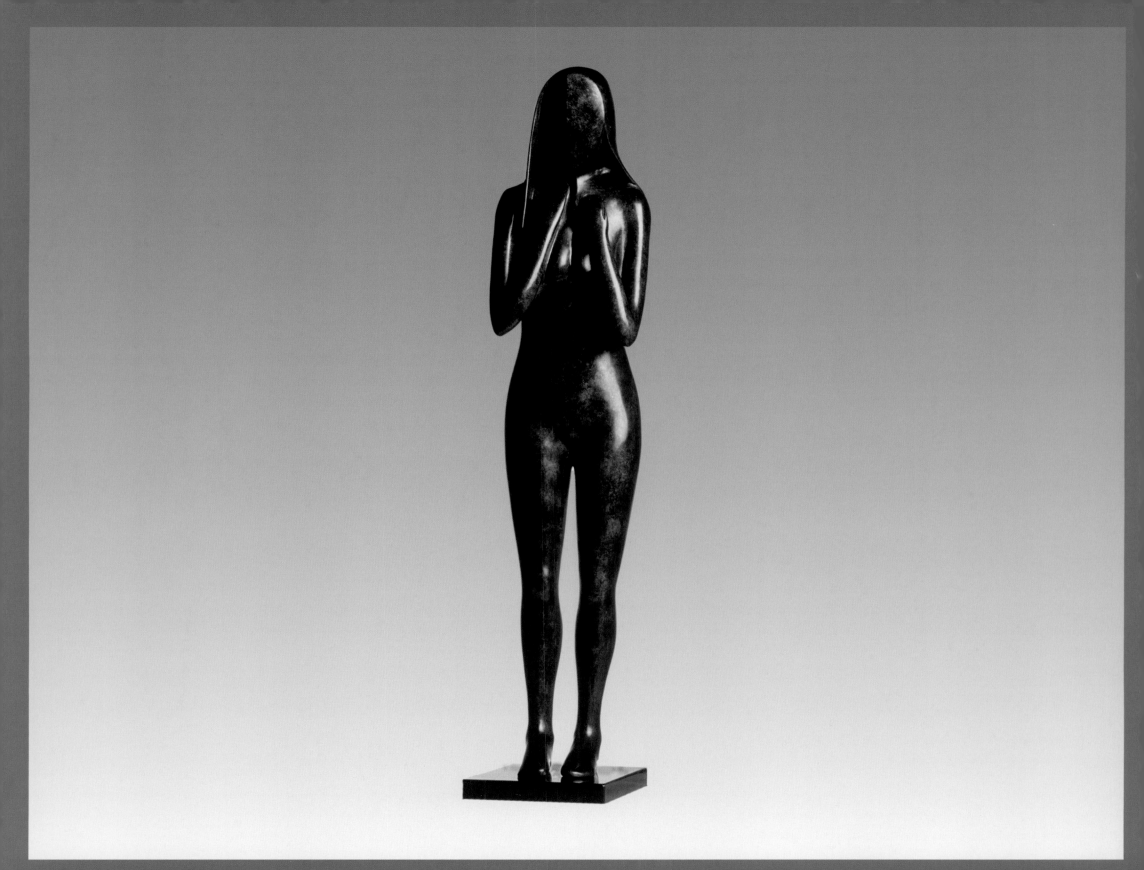

Standing Nude
28 x 4 x 3" Bronze Edition of 9

Shy Girl 1
19 x 4 x 2" Bronze Edition of 4

Shy Girl ll
10 1/2 x 2 x 2" Bronze Edition of 5

Standing Man
11 x 5 x 3 1/2" Bronze   Edition of 4

Thinking Man
23 x 6 x 4" Bronze Edition of 3

Plant

22 x 5 x 5" Marble

Plant

55 x 22 x 22" Bronze Edition of 9

MORSE BOOKS is the imprint of designer/photographer Jonathan Morse. Known as the "artist's artist", he is a graduate of Harvard College and the Havard Graduate School of Design. He lives in Sag Harbor where he does fine art and commercial photography, graphic design, limited edition fine art and photographic printing, and publishes fine art books.

Eric Ernst is a painter and writer. Born into a family of painters, (he is the grandson of Max Ernst, and the son of Jimmy Ernst), he is a graduate of George Washington University with a B.A. in Japanese Studies. He has lived in Japan where he studied woodblock carving, Zen, and worked as a disc jockey. He covers the very active Hamptons art scene for the Southampton Press.

First Limited Edition of 1000
ISBN 978-0-9835419-0-5   Printed in China
Library of Congress Control Number: 2011960318

Contact information:
 Robert Hooke: robert@hookegallery.com
 Morse Books: jmorse2@optonline.net